Unfurl Passions

Unfurl Passions

by

LILLIE R. BATES

iUniverse, Inc.
Bloomington

Unfurl Passion

iUniverse books may be ordered through booksellers or by contacting:

iUniverse
1663 Liberty Drive
Bloomington, IN 47403
www.iuniverse.com
1-800-Authors (1-800-288-4677)

978-1-4401-2865-3 (sc)
978-1-4401-2864-6 (ebook)

Printed in the United States of America

iUniverse rev. date: 9/29/2010

Dedicated to my beloved Salah,
daughter Tanya that is
married to a strong and loving
husband Charles,
and my son Lake,
their children Ashley, Daeshon and Gabrielle;
De'Angelo and Tamrion, respectively
last but not least my dearest mother, Bettie Ford
and late father Ceaser Ford

Also our dearest friend Nisa

Table of Contents

Nature

Angels

Spiritual

Love/Romance

Death

Forward

Unfurl Passion is a collection of poems similar to the body anatomy of a rose. Romantic and artistic passion, which are like rose petals in the wind. Also, they are like ripples of waves on the ocean, forever changing. Love is in the earth's wind and fire, where daydreaming is as my keen inner eye, in other words, directed by Muse, even, my reliable companions' dramatic love and truth. My utmost passion is pastoral and idyllic poetry along with dancing movements of words as I listen to music, for music stimulates me and my inner most thoughts. Each line that I composed brings out a message of life. This comes naturally, even like the single touch and sight of a beautiful flower.

Now, for reflection and introspection, these poems encourage a person to gain a glimpse or even gain a sense of gratification, of a fulfillment of life which may be seen like roaming thought which enters mountainous places or forested hills among gardens of wildflowers.

For myself, I lived in the countryside during my early life. There I experienced many things, surprises, which the reader will see and be rewarded greatly through my poetry. I recall during the long summer days, I would often take a journey to a nearby crystal threaded stream was water that was below the embankment of a steep hill, I would place my beautiful feet in its fresh water of imagination along the sandy places and experience the delight of tiny fishes and the many eddies up against my fervent senses. Also, nearby where we lived, in the pastures there were large Buffalos amidst the prancing horses, each in its own group. I would watch them for hours as they grazed, played, and often fought among themselves. They seemed like human beings in a lot of ways. On occasions, I would get chance to touch them momentarily caressing them as I ran my fingers and hands along their fur coats, they accepted me as if I was one of them. On another occasion, after, I had befriended one of the horses, a mustang I had attempted to mount him without a saddle and tried to ride him but he refused to budge. In fact, he continued to graze in the pasture. Elsewhere, among nature, I had the experience of seeing at firsthand of seeing a wild cub. He was silver-gray. I soon had to release befriended him because of my family, even though had rescued him from an embankment.

I can say that life in the country is so carefree and is filled with many wonders. For it is like living in the middle of earth and surrounded by the elements of nature. One gets a chance to touch and know nature thru my poetry, for these experiences are rich like the touch and sight of a Cocoon that soon metaphorsizes into a beautiful butterfly, bright with colorful wings or as a babbling brook duckling reveals feelings of harmony, tranquility, and serenity; that is, sky and waters below. For this transcendental experience is truly like being on a new planet, even so, similar to being in the Garden of Eden.

I hope that Unfurl Passion will inspire, enlighten, and offer to the reader a chance to enter into "nature", and experience among many delights, amusements, and wonderments of its elements. Also, I hope the reader get a chance to think, laugh, and touch his feelings anew. Other subjects, matters are introduced, such as "angels", "spirituality", "romance and love" and "death". For all these rewards and riches that I have experienced in my life I would not trade them for anything for they are the gifts of God in my life among all beautiful miracles that continued to unfold in my life. These are the things I wish to share with the reader through my poems.

In short and always, I can say to the reader, that a person's goals express both his earthly and heavenly paths. Indeed, as Unfurl Passion unfold in a spiral way, it reveals that one's feet must be planted in the earth, in fact grounded for further things to properly take place, such as wisdom below, and thus above the birds of the air but still being balanced here on Earth that is, light and airiness, intangible and imaginable in the world.

Acknowledgement

I am particularly indebted to my former instructor, Marilyn who taught me my first poetry class, and who inspired and even encouraged me to have confidence in my ability to write poems. Her class was very informative and rewarding, from which I learned much about poetry.

Also I would like to thank my beautiful mother who has been there throughout my life. Her words and wisdom have instilled me with hope and dreams. Also, I would like to thank my deceased father who has been a true prototype in my life: an example to live by, one whose examples have helped me thru many challenges, goals and outlooks. Thank you with much kudos.

I would also like to thank my brother, Charles, for all his assistance and help which he has contributed from his ideas to explanations about the techniques which lie behind the writing poems. He has worked so hard to help me finish this book.

I always feel extremely fortunate for my daughter, Tanya and her husband, Charles for they have been there above all and beyond; indeed, for their many words of encouragement which I received as I wrote this book. Again, I am very grateful for their words of encouragement. Also, I would like to express my love for my granddaughters, Ashley, Tamerion, and Gabrielle who continue to be in my thoughts and prayers. Thank you. I am also very thankful for my son, Lake, who is very gifted and witty, for putting up with me during the long night-time hours, while I listened to pastoral music, while I was writing my book. God bless you and your family. Also to my grandsons Daeshon, and De'Angelo, my thoughts continue to go out to you along with prayers. Thank you.

Here, I wish to acknowledge and express with much gratitude my sisters, Celora, Betty, Ida, Laura, Cassandra, and Rose Mary. Because they believed in miracles, and encouraged me to never give up. Their tenaciousness and durability encouraged me even to be successful. They are all extraordinary in their different ways, angels of differences, epitomized angel of mothers; angel of success; angel of greatness; angel of fiery hands; angel of acrobats; and even angel of love and mercy. They are, my dearest sisters with their many proverbs. Again, I am grateful to each of them. I am deeply grateful to all my brothers who have influenced me in positive ways. My deceased brother Ceaser; also there are Minister John and Woodrow; Isaiah, Charles, and David. For they have been my angels all the times, even in my thoughts and prayers. Thank you. My special thanks go out to my sister-in-law, Debra, who has encouraged me too. Thank you for all of your constructive criticism, which has provided unique feedback for my poems. Thank you for your shared generosity.

Last, but not least, my thoughts and many wishes go out to all of my nieces and nephews; who have given me support and encouragement, also included my special sister Alqzida and her children, Seema, Bebe, Grima, and Tariq; for their helpfulness when I needed it. Thank you very much. I wrote my many a poem. I am truly grateful. In any event, I love you all.

L.R.B.

Nature

The Secret Valley Thru a Maze

"Reminisque",
--- **Wes Burden**, 1995

My heart leads me to a secret valley
The bison buff aloes grassland---in
The mid of the valley, I got lost in a
Maze, while I tried to find paradise
Garden; now, in the process, I was
Threatened by a fox, he proceeded
To be tricky, shady, and then walked
Away as animals in the area, even laugh
Like hyena, and tried to lure me away
Several times, for he had a hastate sharp
Like spear on his head as he kept up
His laughing and the reflection of
The mirror had deceived me for awhile.
It had not given me, the true reflection
Of paradise, that, I was looking for.
Indeed, the fox had kept hindrance both
The furious bear and lion, which they started
To chase me around in great forces as I
Was near the paradise garden; also, I saw
This beautiful wolf that appeared lose
And free, then and there, I fell down on
My hands and everything that I saw caused
My sense of reality to be questioned; in
Fact, the bison buffaloes, the rivers, and
Crystal waterfalls, gigantic fruit trees
The buffaloes berry people and animals
That live there it was like a fairytale.

Middle Of The Earth

	"Evening Reflection", ---**Karunesh**, 2006

In the middle of the earth---
'Tis spring have you ever
Stopped and observed nature?
It only takes a minute
Does, an Apple tree look
Like white popcorn blossoms?
Do, the trees look as if---
They were white, and bloom?
Can, you see the bushes, trees,
And flowers that are all green?
As you move closer they---
Breathe as your breath, alive.
Can, you count every leaf
That move? How often do
They move? Perhaps, like a
Stream of water, even like
Dandelion that bloom yellow;
Also, as a lotus resting on
Water nearby a white swan
And her mate feast in the slender
Thread streams in strikes of color
That lightens, and had heighten
Her squiggly curly feathers--

Wolf Man

"Looking Wolf, Blue River",
---***Lynda Cole/Jan Michael***, 2006

Even for distance in the woods
Passed the silver sand shores,
Out the flowing creeks, I heard
A faint cry for a life line
As my spirit connected unseemly
He became my friend; I touched
His silver grayish fur at first,
And then I saw and touched
His huge white paws in the crusty
Embankment as he, laid lifeless
And his bright eyes raveled
The overhead sky, as the moon
Awaken from a long night's sleep
And I knew and realized that he was
Filled with play some sounds of
Rustling leaves, flowers of shrubs
Moreover, he was truly handsome and
Strong, and dog like, my love for him
Remained forever open and unlimited
A companion that howls incessantly
That is even within the timberline.

A Toad Palace

| "Prism Of Life", |
| ---*Enigma*, 2003 |

In the beauty of speed, in distance
The toad leaped as a Jerboa mouse
The sun bathed her skin enjoying
The rays around the oasis and still
Water and trees, and near her lover,
He croaks from his pond along green
Banks in the deep croaky sounds as
He croaks, she crisscrosses back,
And forth 'til, she finds him there.

Spider Wedding Web

 "Dream Catcher",
---*Ralf Illenberger*, 1998

She set in her web.
In thin tiny legs,
She tightly greeted her groom;
In her silk web
She again expressed unspoken utterance.
Then, he was seen in threads of silk.

The Vat

"Japanese Music Box",
---*George Winston*, 1994

My leap frog moved quickly,
Leaped springing as carillons,
Chimes and echoes. He sprung
In height, to them to flight as
I played a light and graceful
Song, next, leaped in a nimbly
Way, metallic sounds were heard.
This followed by a buck jump
Seen by a quick short plunge
The vat seen on the floor then,
Was heard songs and noises
Of spattering faded to a clatter.

Golden

"Illuminara",
--*Jim Wilson*, 1999

Th' pampas grass is tall---
Silvery with silk panicles;
Th' darning needle dances
With two pair o' wings,
And flatters in her sheer
Colorfulness just 'bove
Th' golden pond: surfaces.

Dance

"The Desert Flower",
--- *William Vincent Wallace*, 1863

A mountain of crimson,
A city of fire Lillis,
Cerise bright red cherries
Burn and glow on the planet
Like the St. Vitus's dance.
Magenta reddish purple,
Sanguinary ruddy faces
And cherry red cheeks
Restrain me ghastly
Like death forbidden dance.

Vermilion

"Mystic Mood",
---***Michele Ippolito***, 2005

Panoramic view of the pelagic place---
Surface bathes from golden tones,
Reddish oranges, yellowish glitters
To brown colors reveal the background
Of a mallard duck; indeed he can
Also sense an invisible painted face
That soon, soon, vanished. O the
Wild mallard continued to drift afar.

Awaking Moments

"Morning Dew",
---*Armand* and *Angelina*, 2005

Ears seemingly eyes sparklingly.
The elements of spring, is here!
O spring has renewed the nature
Of silent flowers in the mist of
Heavy rain that have landed upon
The ground; later, dew is found
On my eyebrows, even have fallen
Upon my wings, even love of spring.
Also, seen in this picture ants that
Continue to perform their special
Duties, snails that torpid at their
Slow peace, while the dew worms
Untangle selves; in short, they---
All reveals the picture of my senses.

Tropical White

	"Cocoon", ---**Hilary Stagg**, 1997

Phenomenal white rose moved, then---
Opened and then fluttered in dark miry.
Hole under a shimmery starry night
The 'twas seen yellow at first, followed
White again, wings moved, opened,
And also fluttered in flight, moments
Later, it found a beloved rock that had
Revealed; a lot of contrast color or night.

Picturesque Ducks And Ducklings

 "Under Shaded Water",
---**Richard Burmer**, 1984

Purl babbling brook was seen over a ledger of rocks---
I crackled with mirth at a huge mud turtle that rested
On a rock along with six ducklings in their birthday
Suits, later they bobbed upon th' waters beautifully;
Soon I lost sight as they then, thrust under th' waters
Along th' tapering spikes; again, they slowly bowed
Their heads as they ascended upon th' surface, this was
Seen by a watchful mother afar in th' sunset, imaged
Upon th' sherimming waters th' darling creatures
For they were not actual lost from my many thoughts.

Indian Horses

"The Brilliance Of Stars",
---**Deborah Martin**, 1999

In pipe dreams we are prone to the ground
In the deep woods, the rivers are flowing
Vertical and horizontal, how did we get
Here? Was it a night walk in a nightmare or
Were, we daydreaming that is in a battle?
Soon upon a teepee roof, I saw shaggy tail
Indian horses' and in the background, beats
Of drums, meanwhile, many Indians were
There, and I noticed after talk with one that
Was the leader; Chief Sitting Bull, for he,
Engaged: in various dances of his ancestors.

Tam, Tam

	"Two Trees", ---*Mychael Danna/Jeff Danna*, 1996

I can tam, tam on my tapping
Drum, but I cannot on the leaves
Of a tree, only the Zephyrs can
Tam, tam her leaves, I can tam
Tam on the low thistle leaves.
Yet I cannot touch her purplish
Flowers 'cause they are bordered
By thistles; even so, I touch that
Painted lady that is on my hand.

Sleeping Bunting

"Green Forests, Lush Meadows
And A Soft Rain Falling",
---**Pure Sounds**, 2005

I painted the "painted bunting" on---
An unbleached muslin canvas as
The bird sat motionless as she was
Sleep, even or perhaps in a deep
Dream as if she did not see or hear
Us in her peerless beauty coat of
A many color. The painted bunting
Continued to rest upon the small
Perch tree nearby inside the teepee.

A Witty Son

 "A Splendid Flow Of Grace",
---***Richard Bone***, 2002

His working place is in jumbles---
And unorganizes; no work benches
Or space therein, but both massive
Things and little things; confusing---
The master-maker's hands stay so
Busy at work, even like the fingers
Of nature that continue incessantly
To touch, to shape, and to mold
The world at large; O she's example!
Also, his world is art par excellence,
And he is the artist: wood craftsman,
Jewel maker, lyre maker, rug maker
And perfume maker. He even made
A water fountain: using a glass cutter.
I saw him once, heard him say like
The thoughts in my head, "There
Is no time to waste, millions of stitches
To put in the field background; so
Slow down and hold your horses."

At another time and place, I beheld
Huge spools of silk threads that
Awaited him, even his Persian rug
That he constructed in rainbow colors.
Next, I saw him about to take up another
Pattern, of his Persian rug skills, but
He was for a moment interrupted---
Had to walk the dog, a large white
Hound with pendulous drooping ears.
The dog stood in attention ready for him
The morning strolled, with his master.
Subsequently, he was straight away---
Ready for another pattern, even to work
That is upon, another Persian rug endless.
Boy! Look at that motif one of a kind.

A Child Pony

"Carefree",
---***Kathryn Toyama***, 2007

"Carousel",
---***Peter Sterling***, 2004

Whiz-bang paint brush is a master work---
He does everything to keep this lad happy
As he paint his pony, he dresses the pony
In a bright hue, high colors and deep colors,
Then, he stroke the pony lightly with his---
Brush, dabs the coat. The lad asked, next,
"Where is my saddle and bridle so, I can
Ride my pony"? The whiz-bang replied---
You must learn how to bridle your tongue.
The boy said "I want a real palomino horse
With slender legs, so I can hand stroke his
Pale soft straw color hair"; now, I have
My saddle and bridle and my beautiful---
Race horse, indeed, he is truly mightiness.

A Mere Girl

 "Graceful Soft Child",
---***Ken Townshend***, 2007

A child, that loves to watch
The solitary bees that, nest
Is; nearby the mud and sand.
Even near daffadowndillies,
Yellow warblers and flowers
Truly in a trail the feet leave
A print in the soft earth mire
That is covered by mud, foot
Worn tired by standing and
Even to walk silently therein.

The Garden

"Dragonfly",
---**Dyan Garris**, 2007

Sometimes, he is funny sometimes, he is
Silly he rest and then he is seen hopping
Under the little green umbrellas in the garden
There are many of surprises, food for
The belly and the belly for food dinner that
Awaits his hunger and thirst and there is
A chance for a snooze in this garden of plenty,
Rich with elements of nature under each
And all of the umbrellas he finds abundance
Of juicy worms; little flies; even insects.

Wickiup

"Northern Lights",
---***Michael Stribling***, 2007

Love is awesome under aurora borealis---
The night sky clinks of many bells clopped
Sounds of horses hoof; while, en encompass
Drummer played his drum nearby a Roe
Deer, had showed off her rump white patch
In nimble feet near a trail of sundew of
Indian Pipes and Bird's Nests a lady in a
Full figure and broad lips dances ecstatic.

Palma

| | "Chinese Sunrise",
---*Georgia Kelly*, 1978 |

She looks strange as an Amazon,
Grows excessively tall and thin,
And wears a flying grassy skirt,
And is noticeable for her bright
Colorful feathers that are seen on
Her head; she bears long reeds
In her skirt: nevertheless, she is
Ready for the winds; she dances
Gracefully with Zephyrs, faster
With Notus that teaches her valor,
While even faster she dances
With Katrina squally to model
Which; is from Mother Nature.

Entangler Redness

	"Earth Cry", ---*Peter Sculthorpe*, 1986

Muddy River puts ashore on
A desolate island leaves fate.
Plummet buried their bodies
In a river churn violently that
Is, tangled in redness, a river.

The Painted Shadow

	"Dancing With Shadows", ---***Ken Bonfield***, 2006

Alone on a creek, trees upon the white sand--I
saw their beautiful shadows, before, I knew
I had painted their shadows in the sand.
The shadows then followed my own shadow.
We were different shadows, they moved gracefully
They show my shadow and I, we, the physical future.
When we turn to dance, twist, and bend; for 'tis
Our ins and outs shadows that lives in my shadow
Like parasol suns shades me from my shadow,
While trees' shadows that conceal my dark secrets.
I love my shadow inasmuch as the sun rays.

Good Morning Snow Drop

"The Lark In The Clean Air",
---***Daniel Kobialka***, 1997

She sleeps expressively in the wind.
Dances with him; swaying her to the ground.
She desires respect around her as one
Poses nearby on an early spring day, so
Give her respect and she will always
Be there. One has to nod and acknowledge
Her for beauty, and even; seen grace.

The Clouds

"Like The Oceanus",
---***Nik Tyndall/Anuvida***, 1998

The clouds greet us as molten looking glass
That is even, as many a wave of the oceans.
For Ladylove called them our waterspouts,
Turned underside; that is, later seen as rain.
Those spotted white clouds, are as mirrored
Lights and they are seen when reeled around
Us, even as a merry-go-around, and at times
They sweep, sway, twirl and turn about us
Overhead, soon emptied 'emselves at rest.
Finally, we are at rest, too! And are seen in
Brilliant light like diamonds; truly, to interact
Like the element of water; so, the clouds
Balance themselves like us and the oceans.

Iris 127

"Sky",
---**Brian Keane**, 2002

A mogul: she rises from
A fluffy white flower, then
Steps upon zillions-zillions
Of Stratocumulus clouds,
Onward passing Cumulus
Ones in circles that extend
Even upward to Cirrus clouds
Of colors, of noon Iris--

Blazing Hot Feet

	"The Moon Inside", ---*Jami Sieber*, 2008

Itty bitty blazing red hot feet from
My mother womb came as a threadbare
No cover or blankets the icy wind
Cool my itty bitty feet that turned
Blue with cold bone chills like ice
Cold polar feet allure as the power
Of attraction the arctic Siberia---
Winds cool my itty bitty feet alright.

Mr. Sandman

"In Dreams",
---***Roy Orbison***, 1997

Blue skies like blue waters say, even lots---
About little castles which are in the sand
Yes, children dance with him who is called
The sandman, for he is all dance and has
Goggles on ready to paint, another sand
Scene nearby little ones children that get
A chance to feel balloons, colorful balloons
Seen on a sand table that looks like hour
Glasses; oh! The red and the yellow sand!
A little boy is next seen, stands on his feet
Then, dances alone, whistles at the sandman
They soon dance to kith, kin and folk music,
And fairytales 'til the children fall asleep
With sand in their eyes, in their dreams about
Fun, throwing sand balloons at the 'man later
He gets a chance to sand blast the clouds
That is filled with colorful sand which causes
Those low clouds to fall to the ground below
And feel up those sand boxes for children.

The Ivory Tower (kiss of death)

	"Moonlight Sonata", ---***Ludwig van Beethoven***, 1808

High pitches and pierced cries heard from grating
Noises that did not bother me, for I can still sleep
Here, in this wild kingdom; soon I am elevated
Even to a higher calling, the cries of shrill, piping
Tones of birds in prey squeaks, squawks, screeches,
Barks and yowls, purr sounds of wild cats, lions
Wild boars grunts annoyance in deep guttural
Sounds; that disgust, I am, then, divorce from reality.
I can sleep even here in my ivory tower pompous,
Lofty tall and elevated on a steep hill encompasses
By a climbing ivory untraveled road, that is in a
Secluded haven, a place to meditation, mimics sounds
In the animal languages bothersome: morally evil.
I can sleep, regardless herein these pestiferous swamps.
For, insects swam in piles, they make music on my---
Window pane like the sound of death, predators thru
The night that is like a deadly lion. Also, wolves are
Like my friends too, constantly howl; they preserve
Purity like a remote escapist: the jungle elephant.
I can sleep here in these woods in the Ivory tower!

On A Branch

"A Woodland Night",
---*David Friedman*, 1997

A tiny white flower revealed
With magical lips
Enigmatic wet-and-wild
Which is winsome, in a meadow
Perhaps, is discovered in woodland.
She unveiled herself
Like a nymph;
Finally, was kissed by perfect lips.

A Genial Native Born

	"Soft And Tender", ---*Zachary Spencer*, 1995

Your love is unspeakable
Like fleurs-de-lis, bells
Lillis of the fields
And mountains,
And those called Casa Blanca
Caused me to brighten up
Like a flame.
You are marvelous!

A China Clock

	"Dance of the Blessed Spirits", ---**Christoph Gluck**, 1762/ 1774

"Ticktack, ticktack, ticktack" is heard
Just beyond my bedroom's window.
These sounds, words let me know
That traveling plants of springtime are
Near where greenery branches,
And china asters are seen. They say,
"Look hall wayward more things
Are known and rested". Th ere is
A crystal cross and unicorn,
And they are besides, nonetheless
The crystal angel, and the little teddy Bear.
For, he wears a pro golf hat; also,
He is seen in Solaris glasses.
And sits silently, nevertheless he still
Is, filled with the tears of dignity.
These things captivate my mood
And I continued to see a panorama view
Of a daddy long-leg that peeked
Inside the window while it was opened.
I longed to hear; besides, he can sing,
And has the mightiest windpipe in the world.
Also, the pussycat is seen in a tree
He moves cat-like, even twitching his tail
While birds revealed their presence
As they flew by and away quietly
I heard my heart beat like that china
Clock, "ticktack"; just then, I heard
Beyond my residence, even the outside
Background noises of nature. Thunderbolts
Clapped and hurled themselves
By the lightning flash, while the winds
Swayed their influences upon the trees,
And yet I cannot hear the daddy
Long legs, nor my little teddy Bear
They both remained mute like unheard atoms.
My love resides with my teddy Bear.

Sad Pooch

"Protected And Nourished",
---*Michael Whalen*, 2004

The adorable pooch, I watched in tears—
In a hora hour, time, as the pooch barked
Whined and yelped overzealously, and he
Then went to the door, and knocked. No-
Body answered at first, even heard him—
His called wasn't, nor anybody saw his
Presence; nevertheless, he yelped onward.
Finally, returned to the quitasol, parasol
For awhile, moments later a figure that
Looked as a dwarf appeared at the door
To answer it, for this little man stood
About 15 inches tall, to let the pooch in.
I wondered to myself, even had thought
Was there another pooch that he, was
Afraid of, had echoed past memories?
The pooch just wanted to play with him.

Orchid: Spiral Bloom

 | "Spanish Reflections",
---***Anewday***, 2006

O goddess, you revealed yourself
Like a flower, fine floral type,
Pouch like pink lips,
A lady's slipper
That intoxicates me
Like red wine and sight
That is, revealed by exotic fruit.

Akiko: Morning Sun

 "Morning Song",
---*John Serrie*, 1998

A morning song is heard
From chirping birds
As daylight enters from the edge of the night,
I enter my soliloquy.
I say I am like the white moon,
A lady that is upon a frost hill
Who, will dress in gay colors
In the night, even, for two?
But will dress in the evening
In dancing clothes that awaits us,
Obviously, we will dress and dance
When the lights are, low.
I say again I am like the white sun,
And I need another to keep the morning
Sun awaken to a bright world;
So, we can share our experiences
In that great city of Alba
Nearby scenes of white jasmine trees
Create the atmosphere of romance,
Even, was seen in open cafes.
Laughter and play is know in the streets,
We entered our place,
Rested our bodies before small tables,
And experience our senses
With the scent of great wines,
And fine breads which pulled at us,
And even carried our eyes
To those who tossed and drunk
From sets of crystal glasses
And shinny brims of china. "No
Introduction needed a table for two"
Was, heard. All in all was said by him.

A Summer's Day

	"Dolphin Dream", --- *Tom Barabas*, 1998

Windsurf from a soft Island breeze,
Sound of breaking waves
Upon the shore surge,
A new star has been born
On a surfboard
As waves continue to swell and die,
That appears upon the sea.

Moon Flowers?

	"Magic Flower", ---**Randy** and **Pamela Copus** 2002, 1997

Levena stood all day in the Sun,
And at night she bloomed into flowers
Thus, she became Rufus petals and petticoat narcissi.
Later in the night, her feet sunk
Into the blankets of the earth
As trillion of stars looked at her,
Also saw her loving children.
They themselves bloomed
Magically into colors of yellow,
And even, blue.

Kopji Hills

	"This Place", ---*Jeff Oster*, 2007

The hills of Africa produced silver and gold---
Their patterns are like Dogtooth stalks of grass
And their fields dance as they plant themselves
Ground ward, to become crops for food for
Grazing animals; indeed, joy to those fields
Of Africa, that veldt cycles of grass aloes rich
In grassland, where beautiful flowers and fruits
Are, in cluster branched along other grass---
Windmill, Hair, Bushman, and Elephant stalks
Of grass soon, they fall like in their season
Ground ward, to become alit by nature's finger
Tips that is seen on hills---here-and-there; all
In all, they are cycled anew on hills of Africa.

Angels

Invisible Angels

"Beyond The Invisible",
---*Enigma*, 1996

Mobility of their wings shades me
From dangers in my viewless
Shadow; she is my inseparable
Companion here on earth rising...

Aquatic Angels

"Aquatic Dance",
---***Vanegelis***, 1997

On a glory day, you go and sit by a pond,
Stream, or river, a shadow of glory will
Greet you at anytime of the day, you will
Feel simultaneously as the angels bring
You messages around the water and full
Of whispers, the waters are quiet and move
Very slowly at times you feel warmth of
Sensation over your body and God sends
You, a gift in a breeze as you were singing.

Talk To The Children

"Angel Wings",
--- *George Constantinescu*, and
Alexandru Nuca/Daksha, 2000

An angel stood in a bow of a window unspoken---
It was the first day of summer. Thunderous, forceful
Violent hailing and rain, 'twas the crystal hail
That had rested on the ground, which looked like
A river in whitest like many angels standing in
Awe even watched, the children as wonderstruck.
The children were in awe too: terrified, and fearful
Of the large hail stones, 'cause their eyes paint
The hails in blue, purple, yellow, and black colors
That had been seen in the sky fallen. Th e children
Also had prayed for a short time as a burst of light
Had, shone again, in fact so bright that the master
Talked to the children that 'twas a sign and wonder
From heaven; do, they understand his languages?
As the cloud close the curtains and darken the sky.

My Strength

 "Aerial Boundaries",
---**Michael Hedges**, 1985

My spirit is free like an ice floe---
That floats at sea. Free as an island
Scarlet Poppy that takes the wind
With grace in her pastel colors
Seen, as I glazed from an unknown
Window, then, I leered sideways
Form out of the corner of my eye
A light traveled like a pillar unto
A doorway; also, seen from another
Window the light of my soul that
Floated around as, a celestial bodies
Even, like dew Heiligenschein light
That reveals my towel of strength.

Transparent Angels

"Snow",
---**Eric Roberts**, 2001

A miracle caught my eyes
Seen from the diamond dust
While ballet angels danced.
They rejoiced in the cold and silky wind.
Moreover, below the glitter snowflakes
That fell from heaven.
As a result, they transformed their garments
Into showiness,
And they who are called Peri, appeared.
They circled around me luminously free.

Angel In Pink

"If You Believe",
---*Jim Brickman*, 1995

Beneath a glowing cross is
Seen fiery flames of a silhouette
As I danced upon the pews,
Experienced in the cathedral
Just then, I saw through
Papery rose hued windows,
A heyday, canopy of heaven,
Rumble sound of praises.
As he carried me upon the curry
Even though there were stiff winds.

Precious Moment

"Ancient Dream",
---*Patrick O'Hearn*, 1995

Rays of diamond dust
Though the branches of the trees
That revealed the outline
Of a vivid picture told about ages ago:
In short Jesus who prayed in the garden of Gethsemane.
The mystery had begun to unfold.
Just beyond events in the earth's shadows
I saw him pray once more
For you and I
As he neared the crimson curtains.
He did not lingered or tarries
But continue to say
He was the Lamb.
Then and there, I knew he would come again
Because he told me
He would return in the sunrise
Indeed he would have salvation.

Attraction

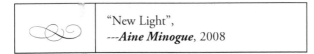

"New Light",
---***Aine Minogue***, 2008

The angels of Venus came
To the rose veil garden
They were undoubtedly filled with delightful love.
They lit up ten thousands of roses
Above all; they used their swords in their hands.
As result this garden became
Like the red sea.

Sunset

	"The Eyes Of Truth", ---*Enigma*, 1994

I drove in the sunset
Everything appeared to light up
Around me in color of fiery red
That came from my soul
Like a cocoon that birthed me
Though the Holy Spirit.
Furthermore, seen
More beautiful than
A Mariposa butterfly,
Although, seen of ultraviolent color.

On Earth

	"Evening Breeze", ---**Esteban Ramirez**, 1998

Angels present themselves
Magnificent in a little whirlwind
Felt as a light breeze.
The nearby still flowers spilled
Their aroma that calmed my soul
As they continued to flow graceful
I could see the frosty hair
Of one of them
Who floated upwardly singing!

A Protector

| | "A Promise Of Love",
---*John Tesh*, 1998 |

I saw a Cherub a drifted in air---
And in her hands a living. She
Proceeded to cuddle this creature,
Even: placed him under her wings.
At this time, she appeared to be
In disarray, perhaps a little confused
About what to do, then she took
Him back to the seashore where
There were others like him, and
Placed him on the shore; immediately,
He hurried himself to the incoming
Wavers of the sea, head was high
Where he looked; his head looked
Onward as he continued: followed.

Cherubic

	"Dreaming With You", ---**Golana**, 1999

Rosy faces, chubby faces glow.
These are cherubic ones,
That is, winged and ready.
And through their peeping eyes
They briefly even in twinkle
Moments, and breathe like
Living beings; Oh feel their
Little toes and short fingers
As they play on fiddles, and harps,
And their smiles bring out blushes
Of pinkness for they are filled
With the flowers of love, even
Wrapped in heavenly blankets
Along with amusements for
Game, song even laughter.

My Mother

	"A Heavenly Gift", ---*Gandalf,* 2007

A woman who draws water from a well
A woman of many proverbs
A woman of royal---
A woman of praise---
A woman of pride---
A woman of virtue---
A woman of worship---
A woman of mercy and truth---
That rises early in the morning, and works until sunset
A woman of motherly wit that counted one hundred and thirty
Toes, and played pity pat on one hundred and thirty hands.

Spiritual

A Crystal Needle Hole

 "Shining Mountains",
---**R. Carlos Nakai**, 2003

Magnitude of blessings is seen
Through the crystal needle
'Tis smooth and in a circle
And become jagged.
As you keep looking for the great
Moment, the crystal needle hole
Circle gets wider and wider.
There is, shout of joy, each
Ridge gets higher and higher
If you see a hill look, for
The mountains and you can
See at the top of the peak.
You are set free upon the world.

Eyes Of The Lord

"Through My Eyes",
---*Chuck Wild/Liquid Mind*, 2003

The heavens are the eyes of the Lord.
And the white thread strings dance
In light as Iris rainbows, they don't
Burn, break, or fade; for, these strings
Are like souls that reach or the thread
To ravel their minds that, are---
Entangled confused, The Holy Spirit
Ravel beautiful lose strings that fall
From heaven free flowing here on earth
Reveal to a soul who must travel
Through a needle eye to see the eyes
Of the Lord; truly, the strings from
Heaven extent our hands to the most
Upper seven heavens where our eyes
Are like objects that travel through
A needle's eye, for 'tis like a way
To heaven, even the eyes of the Lord.
Every eye shall see him and know him.

A Fallen Star

"Inner Peace",
---*Mike Wall*, 2007

My eyes rested exceeded like---
Glory above the earth and heaven
A star has fallen from heaven
Sweetly, it let me know that I am
Beautiful in the site of God, as
I walk alone I walk alone with
God forsaken by most of my friends
Ill favor, unattractive, objectionable
Everywhere altho I look for no answer
I am like a piece of jewelry in God's
Holy eyes it doesn't matter how I am
Forgotten I know I am glad I found
God as my Personal Savior even
Despise by young children in my eyes
So let my life set on the eyes of the lord
I shall do great things I have witness
The fallen star; seen from heaven.

An Endless Road

"Eternal Sunshine",
---**Peter Kater**, 2005

Who will comfort the unrested souls?
Where will they go, and who will receive
Them, and who will feed them and cloth
Them, for I know for they can rest,
Sleep, and find refuge of God in the bosom
Of Abraham, from him who walks in
Darkness and all the unseen arrows
Of death; indeed, I know God shall be
Their shield, tower, and help in times
Of trouble, but they may not know him
Or can tell what shall be after or next---?

Ice Sheets

 | "Night Waves",
---***Dean Evenson***, 1996

My soul rested peacefully
Like the serene waves of the sea,
Frozen and reserved.
Inside thick ice sheets rest is
Known, and just beyond this place
There is the valley of ice bugs
That live and await their day.
Later, my soul awakens bright
Like a light bulb that becomes
Brighter until she is what she is:
Wash clean with hyssop.
Finally, is covered with spices and oils.
I can, then, make my way
Indeed, from this valley and these bugs.
Others will know that I am
Like snow, and embellished with beauty.
And inside this picture, myself,
Is an inner peace where God
Is known, just beyond the windows
Above all, heaven and this experience are.

Lord You're Great

"Radiant Dawn's Whisper",
---*John Serrie*, 2003

My meditation of the Lord is sweet
That is evoked by the Holy Spirit
For 'is like lighting, which pierce
My soul as brightness that comes
Ere my eyes as radiant energy from
Above as falling rain, and hail stones
There is none else can performance
Like the Almighty; immediately,
My eyes respond; he is my Savior.

Vindhya Hills

"Mountains with hills at their knees".
---***Leish Buckner Hanes***

A cloud emptied her beauty upon
The mountains in a glimpse, while
Sirius lingered over th' white church's
Steeple, 'tis light and glow caused
The nearby trees to heat and burn as
The angles aflame hang their skirts,
Then kneel in the dust of the earth.
Soon, my thoughts were a lit as prayer
Is upwardly, heavenly, even reaching
Where, angles are dearest in flight.

His Bride

	"Eye of the Beholder", ---*John Serrie*, 2003

Lord, I will rise in flight wherever
I may be. You have wrapped and bejeweled
Me. Now my soul is decorated and ready
To be placed in a beautiful package
That no man has ever known.

Divine

	"Sunrise Prayer", ---***Clara Ponty***, 1997

Hail to the singing river
In a holy valley
To a heavenly morning
Like rustle leaves
Magnificent waves of clouds
In a wavelike banner---
Sing with him in highly praises
Of rapture---
He is like the river that echoes
To his bride---
Holy heartwarming
Even gleefully---
We give glory to the Lord always
In rapturous and nocturnal songs--In
night scenes on silver clouds, shadows
Of dancing celestial angels---

X24 Baby Xzarria

 "The Child In Us",
---*Enigma*, 2004

A tyke child that has umber light brown hair;
Also, with many a talent, she who had walked
At six months, even born with powerful abilities
Like the magnification of a lens, a mark X on
Her body; and fun-like eyes that go, in circles
As she sometimes, uses herself to miraculous
Speak out, for her first utterance was, "Zion"
For 'tis praise, moreover praises, this is when
She played with two small wooden hammers,
That is on things that made music sounds---
Like the xylophone that she soon learnt; then
Played a forty string zither; another thing, her
Acrobat body had tumbled once, seen also upon
A tightrope as she walked along the way flawless
And was on a trapeze, too where she performed
Para excellence; all is all, she is the XYZ baby.

A Tacit Prayer

	"Mist Of A Waterfall", --- **Wayne Gratz**, 2002

The Lilies is at the tip top of the mountain
So, are the feather feet in Mountainous ridges?
I ask you, I pray thee for 'tis springtime
Where the fire lilies are sleeping peacefully
Awake them my heart, is burning in bursts
To be understood without being really open
Expresses silent and later unspoken ways
Without a doubt; Father, I know you sent
A tiny skylark that had ascended up, even
To the tip top of the mountain just to sing
To me sweetly, and then I become soliloquy
As I talk to fire lilies upon the ground, there.

A Shining Light

	"The White Spirit" ---**Uman**, 1995

In the path way, there is a light to my feet.
In my hands, God gave me a shinny bouquet
From the rising winds, a heavenly bouquet---
Now I know the earth cannot darken my soul,
Or even the clouds of uniform, also even
The shade of night time; surely, God gave
Me a shining light that will shine in darkness
Of dark, even the blackness of black nights.

My Father Above

"Triumph Of The Spirit",
---*Margie Balter*, 2007

Angelic voice from heaven draws
Me closer to heaven through
Song of praise harmonic
Words of compassion brings
A message from above the voice
Never late always on time
My provider, my friend, my
Father above I know will never
Forsake me it is you that I love
I will always keep my eye on
The prize; that is, you my Lord.

Jaunty

	"Shadows In Silence", ---**Enigma**, 1996

You cannot run with the world---
Nor move as fast as the Holy Spirit
For he moves faster than any steps
Of a human; indeed, he is the prince
Of peace: purist of all peace to be.
You may believe that your steps
Are very fast, but to him, you are
Just standing in your steps; so you
Just ought to realize and fear him,
Even tremble and bow down on
Your knees; and then ensky 'self
Into the heavens, for you are truly
A theism that knows, the heavens
Above are wide, even as the wide
Blue yonder; in short, my belief
Is, he is the supreme Spirit who
Is, also the author of all things---
AMEN! The Alpha and Omega!

Birds At Fly Halcyon

"Fly Bird Fly",
---*Danny Heines*, 2001

Akanka eyes are golden
They are as eagle eyes
Sharp eye keen insight;
The cries of the baby birds
That had led her to the gold
Sea, where these fledge---
Birds were, even ready
To fly afar in their---
Fledging feathers; too.
Akanka had a sadden heart
Felt they had lost their parents
So, she taught them how
To fly perfectly, even, uniquely.
For feelings of love surged
Thru her as a role model for
Their parents, she saw their
Real needs and God gave her
A golden heart: the golden sea.

Brain Picking

> "In a deep vision's intellectual scene
> Oh! What a scene", Song, Z506/545,
> ---*Henry Purcell*

Who are you to think of picking?
Another mind; a thought to say---
That we are who you are, even---
To say you have said that you are.
For, it may not be you, that is---
Who you think you are? Some
Times, I think you are not who you
Said you are, maybe, you are
Animals, flowers, trees, birds, or---
Some creatures, that are, you. So,
Say they are, for they cannot say
Who they are, you just may think
You are someone else or another;
All in all, one can only say that
He or she is someone, but only---
God can say who you really are.

Love/Romance

One Unique Rib

"Soul Mates",
---*Danny Wright*, 2001

You were made from one of my dreams,
In fact, were ribbed perfectly in all aspects.
I had closed my eyes
Before the Lamb of the world,
Then, slept peacefully,
Prayed some more to the Lord.
I awakened and there you were
Created by him that loved us.
You were just for me, soul mate.
Yes, we reflected aspects of us.
I embodied beauty
Even, had all your dreams
I saw my crimson veil
Moreover, revealed from the corner of your eyes.
Then, I awakened again
And saw this beauty of mine
Come forth from God
Like something from nothing;
Moreover a blushing bride
Revealed her red face
Like a hibiscus flower.
Further, was seen a scene
That appeared to open up
Overhead scarlet clouds,
Enchanting forests,
Overflowing rivers,
And beautiful mountains
That suggest to a sweet indulgence
Of our love
From lips that welcomed my kisses,
Tongues that tasted like honey cones.

One heart beat was known
From our ears, the sound
Heard as a throb and pounding for love.
All was heard his arms, her utterances
And the words,
"May we eat the pink lady apple?"
Then, our eyes open and we stood
In crimson blood, and only to realize
We were home knowing
That now we were one blood
And one flesh all in
All were, from one unique rib.

My Love

	"Love Is Blindness", ---*Cassandra Wilson*, 1995

I will go to all lengths just to be with
You, my love, through fire and water
You continue to be my breath, even
In the morning; then soon rest at night.
Will, go to the farthest ends of the earth---
To find you once again, whether it be,
In darkness, by coldness, thru wetness
Or inside an air mass that is hundreds,
Thousands of miles, or perhaps over
The Grand Canyon, within Bohemian
Forests, swim thru alligator swamps,
Dance upon glass tables, enter depths
Of icy oceans, fly kites to the highest
Places in the sky, even heaven where---
Celestial bodies are seen, the moon,
Orion, or Sirius---for you; are my love
That shinny Polaris that guides me!

Untouched Woman

"A Gift Of Life",
---*Hilary Stagg*, 1997

A beautiful woman in bazooms
Dazzling in white beauty
Her eyes unblemished brown
I could not see her eyes
Or, body move as she stand
Arrest like a picture that was
Mounted on a wall unknown
Untouched by human hands
Never discovered or explored
She was perfect, save, and sound
There. A purist as a vestal virgin
Intend as nature intended to be
The essences abstract of a woman
Her beauty, which is, utmost.

Ambiguous

 "Out Of The Darkness Into The Light",
---***Michael Stribling***, 2007

A lovely lady stands alone.
She has yellowish brown
Butterscotch hair, as though
She had come from a new
Canyon as a supernatural
Being of light, that comes
Forth in a beautiful ray of
Purple to vermilion glory;
That was also seen on her
Finger ring; now, her spirit
Moves everywhere in an
Encompassing---ambience.

One Body

"Quiet Reflections",
--- *Tom Salvatori/Iris Litchfield*, 2007

Momentary our lengthening wings---
Shared one soul, one thought, we were
One! As a musical lamp, the wind blew
An evening phase from the sea, a light
Kindred our relationship and built a fire
Within our love; oh, like a kindly sun
Above our body, now created afraid---
To turn and be in love, even to kiss
Scarlet lips, even my lips, ended, moved
And I could not feel your breath, only
Your kindles wings were felt nearby!

Spiral Bloom

	"Heavensent", ---***Osamu Kitajima***, 1986

Beauty bloomed in a woman
Three dimensions: her heart speaks
In a quiet place, her thoughts are silence,
And her touches become cloak-and-dagger.
She is God's gift to man.

Twist

"Looking Through The Broken Window", ---**Lucie Silvas**, 2008

She sees a soul through her eyes---
Now, this mutual oversweet, even
Over warm us as a fiery blossom.
Hot-blooded; cackles from my heart.
For 'tis as a knit of thread that ties
A knot, that nestles in a cozy blanket.

A Craved Statue

"Overheard In a Dream",
---*Hilary Stagg*, 2006

The tree is tall and have---
Many wide branches as a log
No leaves no bark sleek
And many statues were tall
And short in imperfect
And I saw one that was
Perfect, and man shaped
In the tree and I wanted
To bring it home as a living
Being so, moment later
He became that being that
Is alive, moving, and acting
Then, surprisingly with his
Right hand he reached,
And touched my left hand
And then, I immediately
I knew he was truly real,
And he smiled likewise.
He was handsome, also,
Candid: even kind, too.
Later, I asked my friends,
Do you want a man that is,
Carved from the hands of
God; hands are truly gently.

My Dreams And Diamonds

	"High Places", ---*Martin Franklin/Tuu*, 2001

As I wonder into the heavens,
The stars unfold themselves,
And then my eyes to sleep---
O peacefulness is found in
This dream, your heart, once
More in the depths of the sea
You were close to me as my hair,
Even a lit my heart free, bright.
Dreams that were seen at last,
You buried my diamonds, one by
One in my heart as a treasure;
After all they can only be seen
Thru the lens of the microscope
Throughout, even a new moon.

Blue Bells Of Fate

 "Messengers On The Wind",
---***Robin Miller***, 1996

A speech with a voice like a thousand trailing
Bells that felt at night time such scene over
Whelmed me with excitement also a red letter
Had followed too, then silence was experience
And stillness with much quietness came, oh,
Even, the atmosphere was very heavenly a low
And soft utterance was none, when he touch
My hand he informed me, whisper "Will you
Marry me"? I respond by the ordnance "Yes---
I will" I was then sweep in arms of a white
Knight through a gentle wind, had soon come.

A Swan White Feather

"Dream Come True",
---*Hilary Stagg*, 1997

We have touched
The pure white feather
The mute swan
A secret power made
Our dreams come true.
Bridal wreath umbels of small white flowers
Borne, in spring,
But, is a token to you.
A bouquet sweetly fragrant
Furled edge
White Lillis for your glorified body.
Nothing is able to stain,
Even, what is called the beauty of our souls?
You are my precious one.

Nuptials

 "Asleep Beneath The Moon",
---***John Fluker***, 2006

My husband you are mature, thoughtful
And understanding, a stout hearted man
Who is straight forward, you are my---
Evening knight on a white horse that
Has a castle in the air upon a mountain.
To my wife your soulful eyes express
Deep feelings and emotions, you light
My heart with the fruit of your hand
And love your household that is in silk
And your strength that is being honor

Becoming One

| "One", |
| ---*Hilary Stagg*, 1994 |

Compliments do embodied our souls
As an oracle; for I can say that a quiet
Smile with a tear is special. You kiss
Me as fruit, even like rich lips ready
My soul becomes, pompously alive---
Soon our hearts tremble as one, then
We become tangential with our bodies;
Species that are in our souls exploding
Inwardly, then outwardly into many
Fragments, the euphonic types of many
Voices; next, the fruit of my eyes
And my mouth, are yours. Yes, even
Agreeable to our ears, yet like peal---
Thousands of bells, that caused people
To turn and look at us, even as you
Sing a beautiful song with melodies
That bathes our souls onward forever.

Sinuous Bouquet

	"The Eternal Day", ---***Hilary Stagg***, 1994

"No more lonely nights to bear
My beloved," Sun Thyda, said
As she winded herself in radiant lights,
And bathed herself in fragrant oils
For men, to blaze and cause them
To shake with yellow passion
Indeed in a sinuous kiss.

Turn Turtle

	"The Tortoise", ---***Don Harriss***, 1987

Women show off, what is on
Their left hand, finger ring---
For even their left foot, toe
Always get them in trouble,
Especially, older woman cause
'T is not like a heart throbbed
But, 'tis like a heartwarming.
Women soon seem to turn turtle
Tipsy over wearing things
That is, too long or perhaps
Like high heels; also, they may
Be encouraged to start and wear
Fancy bright colored clothes
That may be smaller, shorter
Even, prettier than their past.
Such coloration that looks---
Metallic in all its aspects, rubs
Up and that makes men world
A turn around: not as women.

Attract Utterance

"Beautiful",
---***Ryan Farish***, 2004

Bring me a buttercup yellow bouquet
Ten thousand more, closer, at heart
And second let your eyes outburst in
Bright yellow in millions of suns
Yellow is the color of your eyes that
Shows beauty in each soul yellow
Exchange ideals from the your eyes
That reveals readily quick! Alias!
'Tis thru the eyes that win's my heart.

Of A Woman

	"Floating", ---***Ad Dios***, 2001

A fashionable woman from the west,
Is like Zephyrus from a fresh breeze.
For her clothes are, light revealing as
She dances, moves, and then swishes
Her red dress gracefully like a singing
Bee, is, about to leave colorful flowers.
O she swings dance; moves as a force
That is in fact like sound, whistling in
Speech of sound that reveals: sibilance.

The Sea Breeze

	"Sea Of Dreams", ---*Hilary Stagg*, 1998

Nothing but a breathless silence spoken
By a sweet embrace awaken my love
From creaseless entrapment of memories
Alluring echoes of your vicarious voice
Taunt me captivate by passion of your spirit
My heart desire trembles in the presence
Of your being, let us step into the unknown
As we soar our love space my love indulge me
In passion of our love consume me I am
Lost in the existence of who you are sensuality
Escalate, passion invades reality we call life
Gaze into windows of my love, our soul
Become as one, your hands are as a cool sea
Breeze on a summer's night I was found in
Zealous kisses we exchange and I was
Awaken with a gift, a treasure I will cherish
Forever, I love you my sweet king forever.

A True Paladin

"Soul Doors",
---***Hilary Stagg***, 2006

I perceive you like exceptional man---
Perfected in the image of God; I see
Potters, clay being molded in the master's
Hands, when I look into your eyes
I am caught up in the beauty of who you
Are; I see someone very special who adds
Substance to my life; every intricate detail
Of your whole being is defined as perfect
By the uncompromised word of God---
Created flawless in the eyes of the father,
I am in awe of you. I am left speechless,
And breathless as I reflect on God's great
Amazing masterpiece that is, thru my eyes.
The fault line that once crossed my torrid
Heart had been freed by your presence
As an earthquake that opened my heart to love
Your presence causes an earthquake to tremble
Within my spirit shaken my sense of love
Were, awakened from an unconscious even
Comatose state; you set my heart ablaze
Like the wild fires of the forest. The sweetest
Sound I know, is when your voice echoes
My name, for 'tis more than just a mere
Mirage, for I have traveled many a thousand
Miles, have finally stumbled upon my oasis.

Pentacle

| | "A Dream Twilight",
---***Hilary Stagg***, 1994 |

Love is around, th' obelisk pyramid---
'Tis like an oasis, a hiding place for
Lovers under th' magical stars which
Facsimiles; even, as an Oriental topaz.

Confluent Together

"Simple Beautiful",
---***Hilary Stagg***, 1986

As we watch from the mirador
Across the sea of Jazer, our eyes
Become as mire to each other,
Promptly, theses phenomenal
Waves shine tremulous sparks
Of lights; in fact, we finally---
Come together and blend as one
As we all flow collectively only
That mutes in twinkle of an eye.

Each Day

"The First Light Of Dawn",
---*Cynthia Jordan*, 2006

He thrills me with his musical self---
My world becomes excited, and then
Unbowed; truly, he is head up his world,
And is lordly too, being with him, is
Like spring time, regardless of summer,
Fall or winter time; he is my all in all.
Oh he fascinates me, captivates me,
And hypnotizes me; for, he is pleasing
And highly delectable, even more then
Delights of dreams, or wishes in spring.

Springtide

"The Wild Swans",
---***Michael Atkinson***, 1999

Our love is like a rolling wave that
Is seen on the sea, alternating sides,
Reverberating billows, and resounding
Tunes that play re-echoed pictures,
Filled with undulating messages of
Gentleness, then sinuous motions of
Our love; Oh! Is; the sound of birds.

To Rest Awhile

	"Waves Of Time", --- *Terry Oldfield*, 2007

Miles and miles I treaded along the seashore
Warm air from the wind
Blowing upon the water chilled my body
And when I crossed the morass, soft wet ground,
Phenomenally little bells shaped as a trumpet
Full abloom, it is where a little bird sings.
I hesitated for a moment to take a rest
In the present of hundreds of seagulls
That was observed in stillness rest position as praying.
Peace remained here as waves displayed
Their beauty and formation on the water,
While trees waved back to me whispering a song
And quietly jets skis and boats leaped up.
Then, I looked at the sunset mountains
Bathed in dark ebony clouds and in back of us
A red sun face faced in a circle of dark ebony
A peaceful wind, wave, and water revealed
Morning glories have ceased their trumpet
Lips from the dew of watery wave;
Wind you allow me to rest for a moment
And on the sea shore...

Core Of Our Souls

"A Voice In The Night",
---*Hilary Stagg*, 1994

You warm th' cockles of my heart.
There, you touch depths of my soul
Where our love; is found immortal.
Ne'er will we be lost again! We are
Free, even 'til th' end. So awaken souls
Experience th' gift of our 'e'er love.

Thoughts

"No Turning Back",
--- **Wes Burden**, 1995

A purple gallinule had sung his song
About a purple evening star
That caused me to fall in love.
A fresh scent of lavender,
A mountain at the end of a lake
Gave us a chance to soak our bodies
In purple sheets:
Revealed like a birthday type suit.
Again, lavender candy
And lavender sachet filled our room along
Creating thoughts of craze
That welcomed our body home
Then, seen like flowers in May.

Power Of Affinity

 "Rain Is Falling",
--- *Wayne Gratz*, 2002

I love Verbena superfluity
When I hold her in my hands,
When I put her in a crystal vase,
When I smell her perfume,
Or, when I am in her presence
She is elite on a table, in a chair,
Or up on a bed.
Multifariousness is her nature.
She lurid her beauty in several hues,
As in a red glow, she is par excellence.

Succulent Body

"The Perfect Pearl",
---*George Winston/David Lanz*, 2003

A soul was born with a succulent body.
Passion touched hand in sympathy
And true love was seen.
Soul mate loomed in the path of shadows,
Moreover, captivate amorous glances.

Romantic Petals

"Rays Of Light", ---*Hilary Stagg*, 2000

Swift as an eagle…
So, girl, you woo me as I kissed you:
Again we loved on a bed of red roses.
Wow! Your breast adorned me.
Two red roses were as nipples.
Your love was sweet;
Even, cooing me to utterance.

The Bizarre Garden

 "Secret Shores",
---**Hilary Stagg**, 2006

Our many a secret moment together, is ecstasy---
The music played softly like ethereal atmosphere
That gulf, then, enfold our soaring souls, as butterflies
That have alit and their motion are stillness seen
Around the trees, the fountains and flowers until
The bees and dragonflies come, and rested too, even
On the Cathedral screen walls, along the English ivies.
Later, while you pray, soon the presence of a deer, is
Experienced along with a mandarin duck and their
Mirror images, cause much peace profoundly touched
By your soul, that is, as freely flies them; butterflies,
Bees and dragonflies that soar from this garden into
The blue, so will our loving souls ascend beyond
The heavens which have made us lovely in this place,
The mystery of heaven; for, 'tis the pink cord
From above that is carried by you, my beloved, indeed,
Speak softly the perfection of my love. My hands
Are made of threads from heaven that wind into
Red ribbons; for each thread end, makes you uniquely
And lovely and even the touch, requires mindfulness.

Shaddock Tree

"In Monet's Garden",
---***Peter Sterling***, 2004

Flowers bloom in white colors---
Later bear fruit that can be eaten,
Like fruit of her soul? O 'Tis like
Sweetness found in her hands---
A Sweet William that is in pink,
To this end, she shared me, even
With her bloom, whiteness like
A virgin afterwards she blooms.

A Love Place

| | "The Stars, Like Dust",
 ---**John Serrie**, 2003 |

A flashback of your love happened inside
A tee pee that was in burning flames for
Each, and even moment we were together.
When I am not there I hear your voice
Even afar, miles, apart and yet you are
So close that at a later time a new moon
Brings us together in a special place
In the timberline: virgin forest for lovers.

Love Is Special

 "Feeling Divine Grace",
---*Ken Townshend*, 2007

Take a journey through a vision of heaven
It will shower you with love and bring
Our love alive and don't hide a minute,
Second or hour for you must enter
Into the depth of your soul, even within
Your heart; here in my heart, there is happiness
And love, they have bloomed as always.
You can feel 'em, but you cannot compare
Those, if you try to take love away,
Your feelings will still remain as memories.
For they are so right today, and are
Like a peaceful whirlwind. So, let us never
Try to take this love away! Let our thoughts
Just grow, never missing each other, but
Always have open hearts and listen to each
Other forever that is in this love bond.
Soon our love in our hearts will be special.

Dream Girl And Dream Boy

"Passion Sage",
--- *Vivian Khor*, 2007

Your dreamy characters are---
As one night, the male's song
Is heard as a night gale while
His mate sings him lovingly.
Both voices heard Nocturne,
Blending as union in the night
Each: as musical composition.

Whorled One

| "Velvet Morning", |
| ---*Chuck Wild/Liquid*, 2003 |

Green White trees awaken to the sounds---
Of Zephyrus like my words in painted love
Expressions that embraced us; then, echoed
Halloo loud back in an innermost essence,
Even further afar over shining sea waves
As the dance tunes of bagpipes played back
To my sweet awaiting lover, seen nearby
Whistling dudes overhead and under vapor.
Bright clouds appear to say nice loving things.
All influenced the kiss; I kissed two colors
Reveal from silent lips of a Blue-Eye Mary.

Queen Of The Night

	"Moon", ---*George Winston*, 1980

Her brightness is equal to the orb of day
An icy ocean bright crust as zillions of
Souls stare at her as angels that are around
The blue ocean abounds in calmness.
Full blast of winds, Plaon, she reveals
Clearly and vividly full view of heaven
Both unclouded and starry nights---
For the white dwarf stars afar flung as
They gave a gauziness look like trillions
Of floating stars that looked even so
Close to the earth at night, but yet so
Far above, all, revealed as she sloped
Downward in a descend then upward
Ascended that appeared to be sloped
Upon the nearby hills, even, 'til dawn.
She stands out at night as true queen
That is transfigured in the glow of
Sunrise' rays under some Nimbostratus.
Her brightness and beauty is always
Amazing, and breathtaking like other
Elements that is nature, forces such as
That of: wind, lightening, and depths.

Luna Tidal

	"Traveler Winds", ---**Hilary Stagg**, 2006

Wind blast a whistle sounds
Heard from the ocean waves,
Higher and stronger tidal
Swell to become noisy and even
Excited bemused in my thoughts.
Really, captivate complement
The beauty of sunbows like
Lovesome within sunlight sprays
And waves, in fact, are like
The atmosphere of romance,
Or the dream of a love affair all
Experienced under the rays of
Silver shinny Luna, full of half
Rising; just above the horizon.

With Me

"Heart Of The Nile",
---*Hilary Stagg*, 2002

The night wasn't orchestrated
By a sweet melody nor were
I, when we dance again
Waltz with me my darling,
Love me and kiss me truly
For, I'm your belle girl forever.

Belle Elaborate Pomp

 | "Ocean's Chant",
---*Paradiso*, 2005

Array of women dancing in high heels
Their feet speak out, entangle in green
Seaweeds as they move on sand waves
That up do flashiness overblown pompous
Dresses their men in stand up collars
And hair fashion of high mound---
Men shift their women back and forth
Like, as those tall waves in glitziness.

Rara Avis

	"The FireBird", ---***Igor Stravinsky***, 1910

I once saw a tall ballet dancer in red statue---
She was like a beautiful Sequoia---This ballerina
Leaped and turned in her unthought-of tu tu skirt
In a nest: red diamonds and valentine shoes---

Halcyon Youth

"The Mysterious Painter",
---***Laurie Z.***, 1997

Idyllic: a romantic musical scene for all you
Lady on a country side road in pig tails up-do
For a golden feast for a young king and she
Let her hair down and up-do in a pompadour
Spooky scary, hair do in green and purple;
Black and orange; red and white, idyll 'tis---
The young king for a night scene, a romantic
Interlude that welcomes him amusingly with
Laughable da-duck's Ars hairstyle that: do!

Aria

"Atmosphere",
---*Paul Adams*, 2006

Muliebrity is as a true young female on
Stage, she sings her song: joy, peace,
And love as nearby leaves from nowhere
Start dancing letting me believe that
'Twas Mozart and Beethoven I become
Quickly electrified free as air is, in fact;
Then, I dance in the wind, even soon I,
I am not only Muliebrity but also, Arietta.

Magnetic Personalities

 "The Happy Couple",
---**Michael Hedges**, 1981

Grasp tight to my hands for
I am like a magnetic field.
As you draw closer to me,
Especially, a flame is revealed
Of my obsession; truly you
Overpower my loneliness---
I feel while we are far apart.
The live magnet of our bodies
Eyes, even heart exerts power.

Blue Pillows

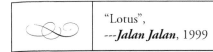

"Lotus",
---*Jalan Jalan*, 1999

The groom perch his bride around blue flowers
Upon blue pillows of waves, they sing a tuneful
Song watching the white, Sea horses play upon
The blue sheets that had encompassed the feeling
Of both peace and tranquility, that were, known.

Nymph Bride

"Rhapsody In Blue",
---*George Gershwin*, 1924

Enjoy your sea voyage,
You are a beautiful one
Love sea lily, small spiny leaves,
And pale blue flowers,
You were born in Neptune's kingdom,
Seafaring upon the sea,
Open water through the sea gate
To the floor of the ocean,
Fluctuating: rising, falling, and winding
That is inside sea flowers.

On The Runway

	"Star walkers", ---*Hilary Stagg*, 2000

In the night she is visible,
Cat walks as the unseen world
Turn purple for a moment.
Then, she gets her chance
To dress in styles,
Fashion in earth colors of nature:
Like the sea, sky, moon, and sun.
She reveals herself uniquely
As a morning goddess
Open eyes of early dawn.

New Fashion

"Moonspace", ---**Tom Barabas**, 1998

The new eye popper fashion a wide
Eye woman wore a Manteith dress
In a scallop hem striking beautiful
And dazzling she is wearing a cloche
Hat in a narrow brim in sepal petals
Flowers the dress is a fashion eyeful
As we watch in awe wonder.

In Pink

| | "Dance Of The Manta Ray", ---*Struart Mitchell*, 2008 |

Luxuriant vintage painted hands and feet.
My lady was seen under a pink umbrella,
Of course, as the night had come alive.
The scene on a summer night was filled
Men who dressed
In splendor colorful suits
In mask faces,
Played soiree music
Over the seaside hotel
Until shining lights were seen,
And approaching twilight revealed
The background of stars;
Now, was seen far above stratus clouds.
Earlier was recalled an evening party,
Where people danced promenade:
Skilled folk, square, and hip-hop dances.
The men serenaded their women with pink wines,
As the night progressed events got more hipped.
The women introduced new fashion,
Decorated chignon purple threads
As they danced in chiffon, sheer pink skirt,
And floating tops
That revealed swaying hands and dresses.
My lady of love in pink
And solar glasses worn
Sparking ankle bracelets,
Painted hands and feet,
Hair mingle in purple threading sways
In the wind
As she danced in the night
She remained gentle, soothing,
And caring
Certainly, she was my lady in pink.

Union

"Perfect Evening For Flying Carpets,
---*Kevin Braheny/Tim Clark*

Our love is like pictures, for you can see
My face plainly as my eyes light up, for
It reveals much of our passion as a rainbow
That is in the heavens; indeed, it clearly
Says something about our understanding
'Tween ourselves, third eye, we are in love!
We were shaken again, even portrayed
By the color of blue, for angelic spirits
Had, ministered to our very athirst souls
Once more; afterward, by God's secret
Our eyes did shine brightly than ever.
His presence is pure love. In fact it had
Effect us, caused our senses acuteness.
Love truly flows as live breath of flames
Pillars of fire, which burn on and on
Endlessly; also, spreads as aeriforms
Upwardly heavenward, even touches
Spirit, too! As well, 'tis like water that
Is in our souls, moving and attempting
Rest; earthly as love in a solid union.

Electricity Ignite

"Spice Of Love",
---*Scott Huckabay*, 1997

A glorious feeling, hair strings
Instead, had enmeshed against your face
While your mouth experienced savor of red wine,
And nose perfumed scent of Arabia women.
These things lit your soul up in sheets of love,
Oscillating from blue, to pink,
And then to red with filled you
With passion
As you feathery stroked my body
So, I would go into combustion.

Neptune Sea

	"Goldstone", ---*John Serrie*, 2003

Revealed; yourself to a sun mirror
You are a beautiful jewel
That tickles my fancy
Revealing everything
Faces vizarded into my mirror
Silk stocking flesh pink
Our souls bloomed together
Like cotton candy
Above the pink sand, letting
The daylight, come in for a new treasure.

Photo In A Dew Ball

"Memory",
---*Carlos Pacini*,1998

Your dimensions were seen
Even, disclosed by a magical dew ball.
A magnetic moment, an attraction has
Alluded, me to this point of phenomena,
And even a visionary has loomed the visage
Of your face: eyes, nose, chin, and lips.
Their expressions had permeated
Through what was called the medium.

Canopy Sunburst

"Princess",
---***David Arkenstone***, 1987

Under the canopy a "bul" "bul" sung to me.
I peered through the leaves
And branches, and saw incoming sunrays.
And then, I kissed her painted cup lips
Just over the bosomed of her breath.
She is like the air that brings life,
As the leaves that nourishes me,
And as the marine that gives seafood.
I will pine away without her love
Like the fading song of the nightingale
"Bul" "bul": through the night.

Death

Swan Song

"Silence",
---*Jacqui Hunt/Kristy Thirsk/*
Sarah McLachlan/Delerium, 2004

A swan nodded her head
As she rested on shimming waters
While her mate continued
Singing
A melody in a mute tone
That was heard by him.
Nearby, Lillis revealed more;
Then, he, pined away unheard.

Sand Dune

"Crossing Plateau",
---***Deborah Martin***, 1999

My feet nested in a hot bed after
A sandstorm, lost from my company.
Now, the sand introduced me
To succulent sea grapes,
Or was it wet kisses?
That carried me home
As I held onto an inflorescent spikelet,
Although seen bouquet.

Linen Handkerchief

"Emmanuel",
---***Datlene Koldenhoven***, 2007

"Please mommy, don't cry!"
The King of glory has selected me.
He has carried me, like a lamb,
Thusly, has heaven me to his mansion.
Then and there, his angels in hey day came
With greeting, and those who were blue sung
Their own sweet expressed soft lull bye.
Your faint cry freed me
Open my eyes and God smiled.
And I saw in his hands
A linen handkerchief
In which he wiped your tears away.

Dolor Wet Blankets

	"Dark Island", ---*Aine Minogue*, 2004

Themes of dark shadows heard after an avalanche
Over the mountain peaks echoed fairy guns demise;
Subsequently, came in the celebration of the New Year.
Children responded in white themes: singing, praying
And dancing
Then and there were silence and woe
From over the banks where souls now cried
Inside wet blankets.
Those who were nearby wept;
That was seen by the earth and flowers of the field.
They shared our sadness and lost
As they wiped our tears away
And helped us bathed our souls
Of the children who cried,
That was known from wet blankets.

Red Curtains

	"Journey To Peace", ---*Chuck Wild/Liquid Mind*, 2006

Please do not close the curtains.
I want to dance through the shimmer
Of the lights,
Fire and furry towering my Adam apple,
That is, sky high.
Heaven kissed me in the bosom of flowers.
Inevitable hour, he harden my ruby lips
And body, nevertheless, he carried me
To the red curtains.
And on the other side, my spirit danced
With others, and reminisced about events
That had been seen before the red curtains.

Seven Veils

"Voices On The Rim",
---**Deborah Martin**, 1999

Every nation and every tongue shall
Remember your words
That a goddess from the wings of Apollo had
Become a fire angel.
She had burst through the clouds
And was seen first in a red gleaming veil
Which she revealed in a true picture
Glisten brightly and lively.
Next, she was seen in a pink veil
That revealed the heavens and the circles of the earth
Seen as a reflux of flames of fire,
Th en, influx rushed forth
Like a flow of blood upon the wind.
Later, she was seen in a black veil
That was ripped away from her face
And she saw the sea of humanity
Unfold both truth and mercy.
She was seen with a fourth veil,
It was a purple veil that caused her
To pass from one medium to other

In short she was brought closer to heaven.
Then, what followed, she was seen in a mystic veil
And things started to unfold themselves
In mysteries
Even, caused her to transcend herself
Experienced as spiritual ecstasy
Like angels of higher grace.
She finally touched heaven
And sensed the flashed veil with her eyes
She saw pin wheels of light
Circled around her head
That brought her closer to God.
Finally, she was seen in a white veil
And realized she was in heaven
Among all perfect spirits of God
And her soul had been transformed completely,
Even, made over, she was more beautiful
Than when she was on earth,
And now was filled with the Spirit.
She could now go anywhere or anyplace for God.

Play With Fire

"Crossroads",
---*Frank Smith*, 2007

I speak hesitantly as I think.
Even when I sit in my rocket
Chair at twilights, my eyes
Follow his yellowish white
Coat in spots, for his graceful
Looks, then huge round eyes
That looked at me as I stood
Up. At last my hands touched
His cold antlers, the fallow as
Sallow to his place of yet rest.

Bright And Ghostly

---reflections of 9-11

"Out of the Ashes",
---*Aeoliah*, 1994

Once, where twin towers stood souls shall
Stare all times no matter where, the ashes
Of many bodies scattered spirit linger, here,
With my beloved in apples of many eyes;
You saw her from nose to tail shining in
The morning sky like a star, even of David
In twenty billions, and zillions of gases
Th at flared both brightly and ghostly, too.
Sway twin towers flame in every changing
Forms, my beautiful love is glorious, even
Distinctive in appearances her wings, body
Formed stream line shine that was as a mirror
On a cloud, for red rows of seats in soft plush
Velvet like, lips scarlet; she is pleasant like
Serene Rain in the sunset: brightly ghostly.
Aftermath, was like going thru lighten, had
Overshadowed her and would not let her go,
Seeing her nose still crystal through debris
Swaying flames, a bright red, reddish orange
Blue and black flames were like death like
Angels uttered to dying souls a feeling of
Serene came refreshed for each soul utmost.
Stammering words a soul shall never die
Or sleep, the city shall never rest, the spirit
Is bright and ghostly among the wild roses,
Swallow tails, butterflies and song birds---
Had long pointed wings and forked tails.

Fanfare To My People

	"Spirit Dancers", ---*Hilary Stagg*, 1990

Cry unto the mountain spirit of hope,
Cry to the wind the gives treasure.
Play a fanfare drum beat
And play a tom-tom to be happy.
Dip colors made ready horn
Seasoned parades of dances
Sing praise unto the teepee tops,
And proclaim your spirit
Sounded with instruments
Among your gifts bestowed
To your people was poetry,
Included was chant, and music.
Daytime, I am in a cloud
I cry for a rain bird during April showers
Then, offer up a sweet flowery odor.
Rain continued to fall,
All in all, was unbroken upon
My people that was from a holy veil.

Fallen Soldiers

"A Friend's Farewell",
---*Joe Scott/Steve Mesple/*
Larry Thompson, 1998

As the tears role down my face my spirit became troubled
The role, call of the soldiers sung and unsung
Whose demise caused by ungodly rulers
No more boots to wear
No more weapons to carry
No more uniforms to wear
A cease fire is sounded arrested in the flowers of their youth.
The flag draped coffin the twenty-four gum salute
Beguiling sounds of taps
A soldier of peace now at rest in the bosom of God,
Later, he will rise again immortal.

Gem

"Winds Blow Over The Hill",
---*Kitaro*, 2007

You were a well beloved person
Alas who were spiritually illuminated!
Like the angels.
You were like sunshine at dawn,
Also were like an evening star at dusk.
We shall see you;
Also, we shall live again,
Indeed in the great day of the Lord.

No Footprints

"No more flowers in the summer Fields of New York…",
---**Allen Ginsberg**, From Kaddish (I)

Your name is written above,
Beyond the timberlines and sand dunes,
Even, the mountains and seven seas
No footprint is on the black mucky tundra.
You are a favorite child of God
And, were picked from a bouquet
Amber ladybug, cool in linen
Beautiful singing in flight to heaven,
Leaving memories rooted in each child.
A favorite child unknown,
A flower child who profusely gives
Love each day like a furry amber rose
That's spilling aroma
As angels stand in higher places;
Undoubtedly pale pink skies and amber roses.
No silhouettes on the sky line,
Ladybug has lifted her wings
In the wind to an utmost stairway
To heaven, around the throne of God
That is seen by her glorious wing.

My Wings

 "Homeward Bound",
---*Hilary Stagg*, 1997

An angel touched me
Kneeled down beside me
Knocked at my door
And said, "Come home".
My immortal soul begun
To bloom, then and there, he lit
My wings,
To carry me home, brightly,
To his city that rose before me
All in all like rays of th' Son.

Aunt

"The First Winter",
---*Tim Wheater*, 1991

My dearest Auntie!
You are now gone away;
You were unable to stay another day.
O how I remember the times we spent together.
You were like my big sister
Who spoke the truth!
I remember the laughs,
And even the times we cried together.
But now I am left to say good-bye.
Until now the time seems all so brief,
After all God knows those things that made you,
Above all, revealed so unique.
Good-bye, I hate that you had to leave
I have those memories that I will never let
Go!

My Greatest Remembrance

"Solitude",
---***Ann Sweeten***, 2002

Yesterday, we were younger,
Even were playful, and outgoing.
Our aunty was like our mom,
And she was like my big sister.
We would not let her out of our sight.
A glow was in her eyes
She was our angel, God sent,
Who was the best with everything!
She was a perfect mom, wife,
Also she was the greatest grandma...
We cherished her each moment
Truly she was seen in our hearts.

A Hero For Christ

"Angel's Flight",
---*Chuck Greenberg/Armen Chakmakian/G. E Stinson/ Phill Maggini/Shadowfax*, 1991

Dad, you are a prayer warrior who prayed day and night.
To deliver souls in despair who needed prayer throughout the night.
We are proud you in all your glory for Christ.
You stand a hero through eternal life.
When the angels came before day, and carried you away.
They lead you from this earthly tabled lantern light.
You were elevated brighter than the beacon light.
Well beyond the seas and clouds way up high:
Even, higher than the Milky Way reaching far beyond the sky.
Escorted by angels to a place where rivers of light shine so bright.
A hero for Christ, who helped save many lives, has earned his flight:
Even now to live the rest of his life in heaven.

Index of Titles

Index of First Lines

159

Index of Persons